HOLIDAYS, FESTIVALS, & CELEBRATIONS

ROSH HASHANAH

BY ANN HEINRICHS · ILLUSTRATED BY ROBERTA COLLIER-MORALES

Published in the United States of America by The Child's World®
PO Box 326 • Chanhassen, MN 55317-0326
800-599-READ • www.childsworld.com

ACKNOWLEDGMENTS
The Child's World®: Mary Berendes, Publishing Director

Editorial Directions, Inc.: E. Russell Primm, Editorial Director; Katie Marsico, Managing Editor; Judith Shiffer, Assistant Editor; Caroline Wood and Rory Mabin, Editorial Assistants; Susan Hindman, Copy Editor and Proofreader; Elizabeth Nellums, Rory Mabin, Ruth Martin, and Caroline Wood, Fact Checkers; Tim Griffin/ IndexServ, Indexer

The Design Lab: Kathleen Petelinsek, Design and Page Production

LIBRARY OF CONGRESS CATALOGING-IN-PUBLICATION DATA
Heinrichs, Ann.
  Rosh Hashanah / by Ann Heinrichs ; illustrated by Roberta Collier-Morales.
     p. cm. — (Holidays, festivals, & celebrations)
  Includes index.
  ISBN 1-59296-580-6 (library bound : alk. paper)
  1. Rosh ha-Shanah—Juvenile literature. I. Collier-Morales, Roberta. II. Title. III. Series.
  BM695.N5H45 2006
  296.4'315—dc22   2005025688

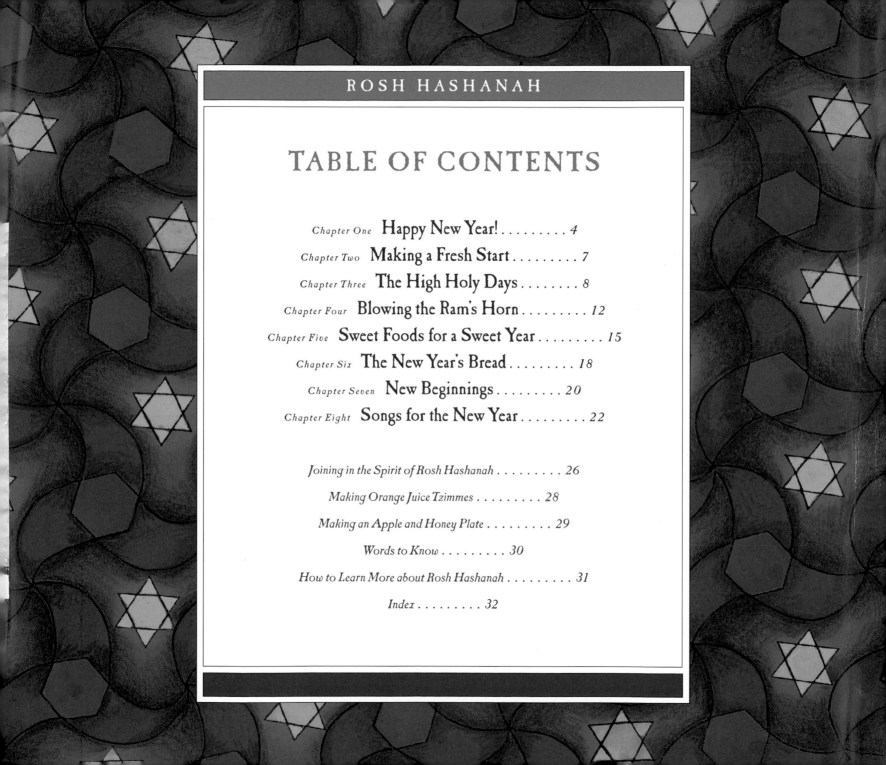

TABLE OF CONTENTS

CHAPTER ONE

HAPPY NEW YEAR!

The horn sounds loud and clear. The table is set with apples and honey. It's Rosh Hashanah (ROSH ha-SHAH-nah)!

Rosh Hashanah is the Jewish New Year. The words mean "head of the year" in Hebrew. That's the **ancient** language of the Jewish people.

Would you like to learn the Rosh Hashanah greeting? Just say *"L'shanah tovah"* (luh-SHAH-nah TOE-vah)! That's a wish "for a good New Year!"

Apples and honey play a role in the Rosh Hashanah celebration.

CHAPTER TWO

MAKING A FRESH START

Rosh Hashanah celebrates the New Year. It also celebrates the creation of the world. It's a time to look over one's life, too.

Some Jews believe that God judges people on Rosh Hashanah. He weighs their good acts against their bad acts. He also decides what the year ahead will bring. He writes all this in the Book of Life.

People think about their lives on Rosh Hashanah. They think of mistakes they've made. And they think of ways to be a better person. People make a fresh start. And they wish for a good year to come!

The shofar (SHOW-fahr), or ram's horn, is blown to announce the New Year.

CHAPTER THREE

THE HIGH HOLY DAYS

Rosh Hashanah is a two-day festival. When is it? Like other Jewish holidays, it follows the Jewish calendar. It begins on the first day of the month of Tishri (TISH-ree). This day comes in September or October.

Rosh Hashanah is just the beginning of a holiday season. The holiday period covers ten days. It lasts until Yom Kippur. Yom Kippur is the tenth day of Tishri. It's also called the Day of **Atonement.** Together, Rosh Hashanah and Yom Kippur are called the High Holy Days.

The days in this holiday period are called the Days of **Awe.** It is believed that God opens three

Rosh Hashanah is celebrated in September or October. Like other Jewish holidays, celebrations begin at sunset the evening before.

The Jewish calendar is based on both the sun and the moon. It follows many ancient customs and beliefs. Years are dated from the creation of the world. The Jewish year 5767 begins on September 23, 2006.

books on Rosh Hashanah. One book notes the names of people who are good and how they will be rewarded. Another book lists the names of people who are bad and how they will be punished. A third book has the names of people who are somewhere in between. These people are supposed to use the holiday season to make up for their unkindness and to start the year off right.

The Days of Awe occur during the month of Tishri. This holiday period is a time for people to recognize their mistakes and try to do better.

CHAPTER FOUR

BLOWING THE RAM'S HORN

Jewish people follow many customs on Rosh Hashanah. First, they attend services in the synagogue (SIN-uh-gog). That's a Jewish house of worship. The sound of the shofar calls them to prayer.

The shofar is a curved ram's horn. It's blown like a trumpet. The sounds are loud and sharp. One hundred notes are blown. They're played in four special patterns.

There are also readings from the Torah (TOR-uh). The Torah is the first five books of the Bible. People offer many prayers, too.

The shofar and the Torah are important parts of the Rosh Hashanah celebration.

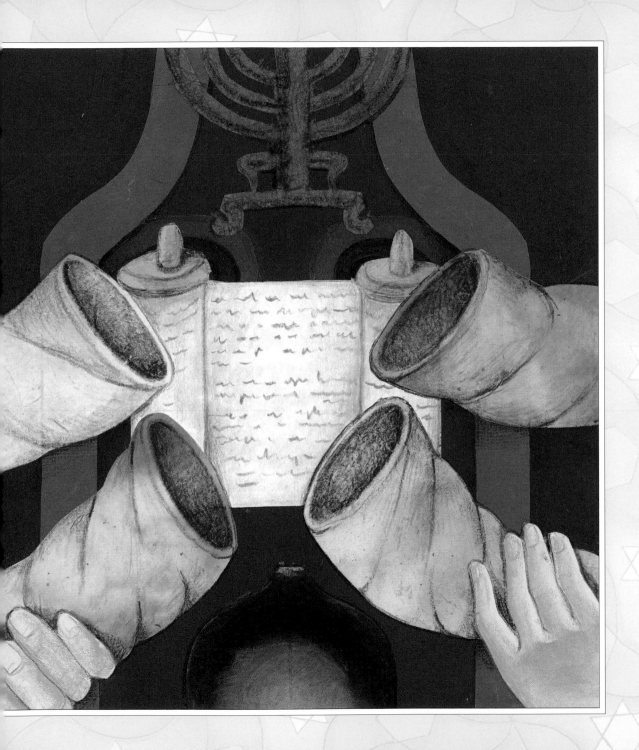

The Bible gives two names for Rosh Hashanah. One is Yom Teruah. That means "the day of the sounding of the shofar." The other name is Yom Ha-Zikkaron. That means "the day of remembrance."

They praise God as the king of all. And they ask God to remember the good that people have done.

Rosh Hashanah is also a time for prayer.

CHAPTER FIVE

SWEET FOODS FOR A SWEET YEAR

Families celebrate Rosh Hashanah at home, too. They eat a special holiday meal. Many of the foods are sweet.

Do you like sweet foods? Then you might enjoy the Rosh Hashanah meal.

Before the meal, candles are lit. Then apples and honey are set on the table. Each person eats an apple slice dipped in honey. This is a sign of hope for a sweet year ahead.

Tzimmes (TSIM-iss) is another holiday food. This is a sweet stew. It's made with carrots, cinnamon, prunes, and honey.

Fruits are often served on the second night of Rosh Hashanah. Traditionally, they are new fruits. That is, they are fruits not usually served during the rest of the year. Some examples are figs, pomegranates, and papayas. Of course, they are sweet. They are another sign of hope for a sweet year.

People say a special prayer over the Rosh Hashanah meal.

PRAYER OVER THE APPLES AND HONEY

May it be your will, our God and God of our people, that the new year be good and sweet for us.

CHAPTER SIX

THE NEW YEAR'S BREAD

Challah (HAH-luh) is another holiday food. Challah is rich white bread. It's made with several eggs. Usually it's a braided loaf. But on Rosh Hashanah, it's round.

The round shape has many meanings. It's a **symbol** of the year coming around in a full circle. It also stands for the circle of life. This is the hope that life goes on without end.

The New Year's challah is baked with raisins. People spread honey on challah, too. These are all wishes for a sweet new year.

Challah is a rich bread made with several eggs.

SPECIAL CUSTOMS

The challah may have a ladder shape on top. That's a sign of hope. The family hopes their prayers will go up to heaven. The challah might be baked in a bird shape. That's a sign that God watches over us in the same way that a bird watches over its young.

CHAPTER SEVEN

NEW BEGINNINGS

Another Rosh Hashanah custom is Tashlikh (TAHSH-lick). That means "casting away." Family and friends gather by the water's edge. Often the water is a flowing river. Then they toss bread crumbs into the water.

This act has a special meaning. It stands for throwing off old ways. As the bread drifts away, people say special prayers. They lay aside mistakes of the last year. And they **resolve** to do better this year. It's all part of the year's new beginnings.

You will cast all your sins into the depths of the sea.
—Book of Micah 7:19
(The Book of Micah in the Bible's Old Testament gives the teachings of the prophet Micah.)

Tashlikh symbolizes the end of old ways.

Tashlikh usually takes place on the first afternoon of Rosh Hashanah.

CHAPTER EIGHT

SONGS FOR THE NEW YEAR

Rosh Hashanah Song

Hebrew:
Shana hal'cha, shana ba'ah,
Ani kappai arima.
Shana tova lecha abba.
Shana tova lach ima.
Shana tova, shana tova.

English:
One year has gone,
A new year is coming.
I will raise my hands
And wish a Happy New Year
To Father and Mother.

Tapuchim Ud'Vash
(Apples and Honey Song)

Hebrew:

Tapuchim ud'vash, le-Rosh Hashanah,
Tapuchim ud'vash, le-Rosh Hashanah.
Shana tova, shana metuka,
Shana tova, shana metuka.
Tapuchim ud'vash, le-Rosh Hashanah.

English:

Apples and honey for the new year,
Apples and honey, Rosh Hashanah's here.
A very good year, a very sweet year,
A very good year, a very sweet year.
Apples and honey for the new year.

Joining in the Spirit of Rosh Hashanah

- Look over the last year. What changes have taken place in your life? Are you taller? Do you have new skills? Do you have new friends or new pets? Make a list of all these changes. What are some changes that will happen in the coming year?

- In the last year, what things made you happy? What things do you wish you had done? What things do you wish you hadn't done? How can you make next year a better year?

- Are you Jewish? If so, what does your family do on Rosh Hashanah?

- If you are not Jewish, do you know a Jewish person? Ask what his or her family does on Rosh Hashanah.

- Think of Rosh Hashanah as the world's birthday. What birthday wishes do you have for the world?

Making Orange Juice Tzimmes

Ingredients:
8 large carrots
1 cup prunes
2 cups orange juice
4 tablespoons butter
⅓ cup sugar
1 teaspoon grated lemon zest
½ teaspoon grated ginger root

Directions:
Slice the carrots into smaller pieces and place them in a pot with the prunes. Pour orange juice over these ingredients. Boil the sweetened mixture on the stove top for approximately ten minutes. In a smaller saucepot, melt butter over low heat. Once it is melted, stir the butter into the larger pot, along with the sugar. Allow the stew to simmer for about one hour or until the carrots and prunes absorb most of the liquid. Finally, sprinkle with lemon zest and ginger root and heat for another five minutes. This sweet food serves six people and is a tasty way to celebrate a special day!

*Have an adult help you operate the stove and slice the carrots.

Making an Apple and Honey Plate

Here's a special way to wish your family and friends a sweet year.

What you need:
1 plastic or sturdy paper plate
1 plastic cup
Nontoxic permanent markers
Glue

Instructions:
1. Use the markers to decorate your plate with pictures of apples.
2. Write "FOR A SWEET YEAR!" on the plate.
3. Glue the plastic cup to the plate.
4. Fill the cup with honey.
5. Have a grown-up help you cut an apple into slices and place them on your plate.

Now you are all ready to share some apples dipped in honey.
L'Shanah tovah—Have a good year!

Words to Know

ancient *(AYN-shunt)* very old; usually meaning thousands of years old

atonement *(uh-TONE-muhnt)* making up for doing something wrong

awe *(AW)* wonder; amazement

ram *(RAM)* a male sheep

resolve *(ree-ZOLV)* to make a promise to yourself

sins *(SINZ)* bad acts

symbol *(SIM-buhl)* an object that stands for an idea

How to Learn More about Rosh Hashanah

At the Library

Blumberg, Margie, and Laurie McGaw (illustrator). *Avram's Gift.*
Bethesda, Md.: MB Publishing, 2003.

Kropf, Latifa Berry, and Tod Cohen (photographer). *It's Challah Time!* Minneapolis: Kar-Ben Publishing, 2002.

Zalben, Jane Breskin. *Happy New Year, Beni.* New York: Henry Holt, 1993.

Zucker, Johnny, and Jan Barger Cohen. *Apples and Honey: A Rosh Hashanah Story.* Hauppauge, N.Y.: Barrons Educational Series, 2002.

On the Web

Visit our home page for lots of links about Rosh Hashanah:
http://www.childsworld.com/links

NOTE TO PARENTS, TEACHERS, AND LIBRARIANS:
We routinely verify our Web links to make sure they're safe,
active sites—so encourage your readers to check them out!

ABOUT THE AUTHOR

Ann Heinrichs lives in Chicago, Illinois. She has written more than two hundred books for children. She loves traveling to faraway places.

ABOUT THE ILLUSTRATOR

Roberta Collier-Morales has been an illustrator for more than twenty-five years. She lives in Boulder, Colorado, with her mother, her fifteen-year-old son, a dog, a cat, and a goldfish. Collier-Morales also has a daughter who lives in New York City.

Index